# Rebellion To Righteousness

HOPE FOR THE NEXT GENERATION

TESTIMONY
OF
JIM LAW

© Copyright 2014 Jim Law

This book is protected by the copyright laws of the United States of America. No part of this book may be reproduced or transmitted in any form or by any means, electronic or mechanical, including photocopying, recording or by any information storage and retrieval system, without permission in writing from Jim Law. The use of short quotations or occasional page copying for personal or group study is permitted and encouraged. Permission will be granted upon request. Scripture quotations are taken from the HOLY BIBLE, KING JAMES VERSION.

Publisher: DiggyPod
Cover Design: John Gill

ISBN 978-0-615-95716-6

For book purchases call 717-921-2622

To: Chaplain Greg Briggs

God Bless You Always!

*[signature]*

2 Cor 5:17

To Doris

This book is dedicated to you,
my godly, beautiful wife,
my biggest supporter,
my encourager,
my best friend,
and after Jesus,
the love of my life.

# Acknowledgments

God has placed so many wonderful and incredible people in my life; I find it almost impossible to list all of them in this book.

I do want to honor those who have helped to make the writing of this testimony a reality.

**Doris Law** – My better half on all accounts. You encouraged me to keep moving forward until the book was completed. You edited, proofed, read and re-read each page until the Holy Spirit was satisfied, honoring what God has done in and through my life. For that and so much more, I love you!

**Jeff Ditty** – The man of God that the Holy Spirit used to reveal the love of Christ to me when I was in total rebellion, arrogant, selfish and not looking for God. I'm eternally grateful to your obedience in reaching out in love.

**Adam Still** – My nephew, although in college with more than enough books to read and paperwork to get done, thank you for taking the time to re-write some of the text with the proper words and grammar.

**Kathy Turnbaugh** – A long-time friend of Doris and I. Our gratitude and appreciation for the many days you sat at a computer typing, editing, proofing and retyping page after page.

**Eileen Adams** – Thank you for taking the lead many years ago by listening to all of the tapes and transcribing them onto a computer.

**I pray that the hearts that are touched, the lives changed and the souls that are saved through this testimony will be added to your heavenly account.**

# Endorsements

Jim Law's testimony is one of the most powerful examples of God's grace operating in a man's life. This book brings to light how far down to the depths of darkness Satan and the fallen nature can take a man and yet, it reveals the abundance of God's grace and mercy extended to man to cause him to be a light in a sin darkened world. This truly is a testimony of one being translated from the kingdom of darkness into the kingdom of His dear Son!

*David Borg*
**Associate Pastor, Jimmy Swaggart Ministries**
**Professor, World Evangelism Bible College**
**Baton Rouge, Louisiana**

Jim Law's life is an awesome demonstration of the power of God to profoundly change the human heart! Only supernatural, spiritual power can bring about the deep transformations in attitudes, behaviors, and values which Jim relates for us here. I am a psychologist devoted to all dimensions of human development and transformation; both my research and fifty years of experience in treatment and education bears this out. Such rapid and pervasive renovation of the heart can come only with and through the Holy Spirit.

*Lois A. Dodds, Ph. D.*
**Psychology and Human Development**
**President, Heartstream Resources**
**Liverpool. Pennsylvania**

From rebellion to righteousness is a personal testimony of how God has used Jim Law to reveal that no matter how bad our situation is, God can turn it around and use us for His glory. Jim got a second chance by living and walking in faith which brought him out in victory to share the gospel and give hope to the next generation.

*Dr. Thomas R. Horn, D.C.*
**Horn Family Chiropractic and Co-author of the bestselling book;**
**7 Wellness Secrets That Will Change Your Life**
**Athens, Pennsylvania**

The personal testimony of Jim Law's life is truly one that proves that God's love and grace for all mankind is real. Truly this is a beauty for ashes story that gives hope to all who are lost and feel that there is no hope for them at all. Jesus truly came to seek and save the lost and this is a heartfelt testimony of a man coming to the end of his rope and reaching out to the living God of heaven for forgiveness, salvation, and total restoration. This is a must read soul winning tool for all who need the true and living savior.

*Tony Townsend*
**Senior Pastor, Faith Community Fellowship**
**York, Pennsylvania**

Jim Law's story is exciting, challenging and inspiring for anyone who is looking for the truth and reality of God. The accounts of Jim's early life, unhappy childhood, his search for inner peace and then his turn and total surrender to Jesus will not only inspire you, if you have lost hope, but lead you to the only one who can give peace, Jesus Christ. This is especially a great book for all parents who have lost hope for their children ever turning around! God truly is still doing miracles. Jim Law's life is a miracle of an ever loving God.

**Dee Cashman**
**Senior Pastor, York Christian Fellowship**
**York, Pennsylvania**

When I first met Jim Law I saw a man totally committed to criminal activity who lived his life in a state of rebellion. I have had the privilege of seeing God transform him into a new person who has become a faithful servant of our Lord and Savior Jesus Christ. I am confident that God will use Jim's story to reach multitudes of people who need to hear and understand the life changing power of the Gospel. I believe God will use this book as a ministry in prisons and other locations in every state throughout our great nation.

**Jeffrey Ditty**
**Former Acting Superintendent, SCI Camp Hill**
**Camp Hill, Pennsylvania**

# TABLE OF CONTENTS

## FOREWORD

## INTRODUCTION

1. Born Not into A Garden Of Eden ... 1
2. The Black Sheep Syndrome ... 5
3. Eating From the Forbidden Tree ... 11
4. The Fall and Its Consequences ... 19
5. The Wilderness Years ... 25
6. Fear of Death ... 31
7. My Burning Bush Experience ... 37
8. God's Patriarchs ... 43
9. Ministry Begins and the Riot Erupts ... 45
10. The Exodus – Freedom At Last ... 51
11. The Blessings and Favor Of God ... 55
12. Hope for The Next Generation ... 61
13. Salvation Prayer ... 63

# Foreword

Quite frequently we raise the questions: What has gone wrong with our society today, what has caused the problems, and what can be done to correct them? Almost daily we hear of school shootings, drug busts, rapes, robberies, and people being threatened. It is no wonder that people are questioning the ills of society.

Unfortunately, we have been treating the symptoms and the effects rather than the causes. We have been putting a band aid on the problems, with more prisons, more police on the streets, metal detectors in our schools, and a host of other safeguards that do not effectively cure the problems of our society.

To get to the bottom one must acknowledge that the basic reason for the cause is the self-centeredness of mankind. When, in the garden of Eden, Adam and Eve turned from being God-centered to being self-centered, it set the pattern for all the sins and problems of the world to this day. **(Romans 5:12: "Wherefore, as by one man sin entered into the world, and death by sin; and so death passed upon all men, for that all have sinned.") In *Jeremiah 17:9*, God said,, "The heart is deceitful above all things, and desperately wicked; who can fathom it?"** The sins in the heart of every person have produced the problems we face today.

Yet, there is hope for the next generation. As there was hope for me and my generation, there is the same hope for you, your children, and your grandchildren. But this hope is not coupled with the entitlement mentality that has gripped the minds of the people in our country; this hope is not bought with money, power or congressional earmarks. This hope is the only answer to a dying, unholy and sinful world. This hope, as you will see after reading this book, is as real as you and I are at this moment.

If you've ever needed hope in your life, have reached the end of your rope and did not know where to go, turn the pages of this book and read with expectancy and faith that there is a God and He is very much alive, desiring for you to believe

> **THERE IS HOPE FOR THE NEXT GENERATION**

and hope in Him for not only this life on earth, but for the rest of eternity with Him.

# Introduction

"Mr. Law, you are a menace to society. You cannot be trusted around anyone or anything. You have total lack of regard or respect for life, or for anyone's property. You live your life just doing whatever you well please. You have destroyed other people's lives with the drugs that you sell. You have shamed not only your family, but anyone you come in contact with.

I hereby sentence you to no less than eight and a half years to no more than seventeen years in the State Correctional Institutes of Pennsylvania. Mr. Law, I hope that you take this time to reflect and do an examination of your life, because if it was up to me, I would see that you would never be allowed out on the street again."

I stood there, looking intently with cold eyes, glaring at the judge, everything within me mustering a hard exterior, trying to show that I did not care what he said, or how he said it. Inside, my heart sank, my knees were trembling, and thoughts of suicide were flashing through my mind.

After the sentencing that morning, right there in the courtroom, they handcuffed me, shackled me, then took me to the basement of the courthouse to a holding cell where I sat staring at the walls for what seemed like an eternity. But in reality it was just a few hours.

Later that afternoon when all of the courtrooms business was completed for the day, I was placed into the sheriff's vehicle and transported to the county prison.

When I got back to my cell, I wept like a child. Aspects of my life flashed before me. I remembered that at five years of age my father dropped me off at the first grade elementary school and said, to me, "Son, God gave you two hands to fight with, two feet to run with. Do one or the other. Don't come home crying or I'll give you something to cry for."

Yes, I was not born into a Garden of Eden. I was born into what they call nowadays a dysfunctional family background. Later that week, I was again handcuffed, shackled, and transported to the State Penitentiary to serve my sentence.

> **MY LIFE FLASHED BEFORE ME**

# Chapter 1

## BORN NOT INTO A GARDEN OF EDEN

The scene is Philadelphia — the city of brotherly love. When you are born and raised on the streets of Philadelphia or any big city, you learn to be a fighter, a survivor, early in life. For me, I was just trying to survive my family life. My father was an alcoholic, and there were times during his alcoholic raves where he would beat me so badly that I could not go to school the next day.

There was one instance where I remember being so sore from his beating that I was not able to go to school the next day. I walked up the street to the neighbor's house and when I knocked on the door, and they opened the door, they asked me what I wanted. I tore open my shirt and I showed them the black and blue marks on my body.

I said,, "Here, look at this."

"Who did that to you?" The neighbors asked.

"You did it to me," I told them.

"We did it to you?" They asked, "We did not have anything to do with that."

I said,, "Yes, you did. You're the one's that gave my father the whiskey last night. You gave it to him and he came home and did this to me. So you're responsible for this."

They looked at me in awe, not knowing what to say or what to do. I turned around, walked away, and headed back down the street to play stickball once again.

Let me just lay a foundation and give you a little background information about my family. My mother's maiden name was Lucille Abbondola. She was full-blooded Italian, born and raised in Brooklyn, NY. She was a heavy-set woman most of her life. She was close to 250 pounds, but she was a very happy woman, happy go lucky, just enjoyed life and enjoyed people and being around other people. She worked hard all of her life, third shift at a factory for about twenty-four years. The plant decided to uproot and move to another state and if you did not move with them, you lost everything that you had invested there. So my mother became unemployed after that.

My mother did not get her driver's license until she was close to forty years old and we all had to depend on our father for taking us everywhere. But bless her heart, she did the best she could and she hung in there her whole life.

My father, George A. Law, well, his father died when he was only a few years old and he was raised by a grandfather who took a belt and a licking to any one of the children in that household thinking that was the only way to raise a child. Not by just straight disciplining and spanking, but maybe a fist or two here and there and that would help straighten them out.

In defense of my father, he did not really know how to raise children. When he became a father, there were not many schools or night classes on how to be a better parent, so parents during that time period did the best they could from what they knew. If my father was alive today and raising children as I was raised, he would probably be in prison doing time for child abuse. He was my father and I do love God for using him to bring me into the world. There were times; however, growing up, as I will share a little bit later, that caused me to grow to hate him at an early age.

> **SHE DID THE BEST SHE COULD**

The rest of my family consists of an older brother who is about two and a half years older than me. His name is John and, yes, we're brothers, but we've never been real close, and that's that. He had his friends, and I was the younger brother and had to go my own way. Because he was the oldest child and he did what he wanted to do in life, his world seemed so out of reach for me. I was the second born child to this couple and in Chapter 2 we will talk about the "black sheep syndrome," the feeling like everything is blamed on you, no matter what went wrong.

I have two younger sisters; the oldest one is Darlene, and the youngest one, Debbie, is the baby of the family. They are all alive and doing well. I tried to look out for my sisters the best I could growing up, making sure that nobody on the street messed with them or hurt them in any way.

Growing up back in the late 50's – early 60's was a lot different than being raised up today. Back in the 60's, when you went to school, children got in trouble for things that are normal today: chewing gum, being tardy (late for class), or speaking out of line. They were sent to the principal's office and punished.

Nowadays, kids are in trouble for bringing knives and guns to school, beating someone up, or robbing the cars in the parking lot. What a difference thirty to forty years make in behavior.

I remember gathering around the old big black and square RCA TV, when we finally had enough money to purchase one. We watched shows like Leave It to Beaver, The Brady Bunch, and positive programs like them. Nowadays, people are sitting around television watching shows that glorify evil, mega-death this, mega-death that, movies where people's body parts are hacked off and just taking your mind out there in left field. And of course, we have these nutty reality shows, which are not real at all, it's a put on. Actually, what Hollywood is saying is that these programs and situations are the norm. This couldn't be further from the truth. It's all deception.

If I was hanging out on the street corner when I was a child and I had used profanity or said, something disrespectful, and one of our neighbors would have seen me or heard me, they would have approached me. Even if they didn't know me, they would have said,, "Son, you should not use that type of language. You should not be speaking that way."

**IT'S ALL DECEPTION**

Nowadays, if someone sees someone else's child doing something wrong, they don't say anything. They don't want to become involved, and that is what's wrong with the neighborhoods and the people today. They are not willing to get involved.

Back then, we had many fathers, we had many mothers and authority figures in our lives and they didn't hesitate to correct a child, even if that child was not their own. Today, people are very hesitant because they are afraid of being sued or going to court on some trumped-up charges.

# Chapter Two

## THE BLACK SHEEP SYNDROME

It is sad to say but a lot of the memories that I do have are not pleasant memories, especially when it comes to thinking about my father. There were times when he drank hard liquor or whiskey and was out of control. Most of the time he drank beer and he was not too bad on beer. When I say not too bad, I mean he did not get violent, but when anyone would give him whiskey, he would become violent and it was usually with me, the middle child, the black sheep of the family, the second son that felt the brunt of that violence.

My mother worked third shift all her life, so she was not home from 10:30 at night until 8:00 in the morning. But when she was home and my father was drinking, he would physically, verbally and emotionally abuse her. There were school nights when we as children were upstairs in our bedroom trying to sleep, and also on the weekends when she was not working, my father would come home drunk and as we lay in the bed listening to him, he would call her all sorts of names and accuse her of having affairs behind his back and many other things of that nature.

Believe me, I loved my mother and I praise God for her. But at 250 pounds most of her life, she was not having affairs with men. My mother was very faithful to my father. She was a beautiful woman from the inside out. She really hung in there in a marriage that most women couldn't.

> **THE BLACK SHEEP OF THE FAMILY**

Listening to him screaming at her, and physically assault her, would rip our hearts out. We would lay up there and hear that and just cry inside. Who could we turn to? What could we say to anybody? If I said, anything to anybody about my father, he would beat me.

I do not know what my brother and two sisters were thinking in their minds when we were listening to my father beating my mother, but the thoughts that were going through my head were thoughts of revenge that as I grew older and bigger physically, I would take his life and pay him back for hurting my mother and the rest of us the way he did.

We lived through this week after week, month after month, year after year, through our whole childhood.

There was one instance when my father came home and you could tell he was drinking whiskey. During those times we were immediately sent upstairs to our rooms. He was very unsteady on his feet due to the alcohol and we heard them downstairs there yelling at each other. We heard a lot of thumping noises from downstairs and what sounded like wrestling. All of a sudden it got real quiet and inside me I thought, my goodness, what happened, did he kill her?

Then, all of a sudden, we heard my father's voice saying, "Let me up, let me up." We snuck down the steps and looking through the handrails of the banister; we could see our mother sitting on our father. She had learned when he was drunk with whiskey, to put a leg behind him causing him to trip and fall, and then she would sit on him with her 250 pounds so he couldn't get up. She found that to be very effective and from that point on, for me personally, it gave me a little hope that my mother could take care of herself when he was that drunk and abusive.

It seemed like once a month or so that my father in his drunken outrages would do something very strange which I still don't understand today. He would come home, open up the front door and begin tossing furniture and things from inside the house, out the front door, down into the pavement and onto the street. He would just start throwing everything in the house outside. None of us understood why he did that. But when he'd start to do that, my mother or a neighbor would call the police. The Philadelphia Police paddy wagon would come and pick him up.

I remember distinctly everyone, the neighbors, and the police knew him by his nickname, "Irish." They would talk to him, calm him down and get him into the back of the paddy wagon, take him down to the 14$^{th}$ police precinct in Philadelphia, off Germantown Avenue and lock him up for the night, let him sober up, and in the morning release him. He would jump on the trolley car and head back home again. By then, we arranged everything back in order that he threw outside. After a few days, he and my mother would talk again and things would go back to what we knew as "normal."

As a young child growing up with the type of family life that I had, I was not getting the love and emotional support that I needed from my own family. Because of that, I became dysfunctional early in life and began to hang out on the street early. I began to eat whatever I could get my hands on. I became fat and overweight.

I remember at one point I weighed over 230 pounds when I reached high school age. I was a very chunky young boy growing up. My father would say to people that I looked like a taxi cab going down the street with both doors open because of my big ears and fat body. He kept telling me that I was no good and that one day I would end up in prison.

I had freckles on my face and a short haircut. In fact, my father did not believe in spending money on haircuts. I remember for quite a while there he would give us haircuts and we would live with burr haircuts until the next one.

There were some good times that I do remember. I do thank my father for always being a good provider. He did provide a roof over our heads at all times, clothes on our backs, and food on the table. There were times when he went out and spent his paycheck drinking and come home with absolutely nothing left in his pocket. Those were the times when I really remember my mother not speaking to him for quite a while.

He would take us out for Sunday drives and stop and get an ice cream. He would drive us to the sea-shore in Wildwood, Cape May, and North Cape May where we had what we call a lot of courtesy aunts and uncles, these were people you knew as a child growing up, but not really related. They were not blood relatives, but you honored them with courtesy names like Uncle Bill, Uncle Bobby, and Aunt Marie and so on.

> **MY FATHER WAS A GOOD PROVIDER**

I also remember my father's mother. My grandmother was an Irish woman with the Irish brogue and when she talked, you heard that. I remember that she was a godly woman. She influenced my life. When she came over to the house, she made my father behave and the times she was there, she would bring us treats. She set quite an example. She lived until she was ninety-seven years old. She did not stop working until she was ninety-two! That in itself is a testimony of a godly individual and I hope one day to sit before God the Father with her in heaven and thank her for the input she had into my life.

My father had a brother who I am named after, Uncle Jim. He was in the military for a lot of years and after retirement he worked as a master sergeant senior at Andrews Air Force Base outside Washington, DC for quite a number of years. I remember him coming up and visiting. There were a lot of good times, miniature golf trips, and things like that.

On my mother's side, I remember taking trips to New York and visiting some of her relatives and her sister, Aunt Catherine, in Patchogue, Long Island. On my mother's side, they were all Italian and so they were all involved in some type of business activity…. and well, you get the drift. Overall, we had a lot of good times with family members on her side.

I'd like to emphasize that as you're reading this book and I relate a lot of my family dysfunctions that I'm trying to give an understanding of probable reasons for my rebellion. I want to also encourage you that there were also good times growing up in my family just as I'm sure there were good times in your family, even if you experienced dysfunction.

Growing up as a child in Philadelphia, they had rules for what school you would attend depending upon where you lived. We fell within the guideline of a half block difference from one elementary school to another. The difference was that my siblings along with myself, and just a few other people were the only Caucasians in the school from first to sixth grade. So I know what it feels like to be in a minority.

When you are brought up and raised in that type of environment, you have to get street smart real fast and learn to be a survivor. Looking back, I remember getting into a lot of fights, losing my lunch money, losing my lunch, not really making a whole lot of friends, feeling like an outcast, feeling all alone, not really doing well in school. It is not that I did not have a good mind. I remember back in eighth grade taking an IQ test and finding out I had an IQ of 129. It's just that I was not encouraged to use my mind to the best of its ability and not encouraged that I could do things right and well.

On Sunday's, we were made to go to church and Sunday school every week. We were brought up and raised in a Presbyterian church but I do not remember my parents going very much. I remember them definitely going twice a year, and we all know what times of the year that was … Christmas and Easter. Everyone put on their best suit for those times.

My mother was a Catholic growing up and I remember her Catholicism influence which caused me to attend Christmas Eve Mass a lot. I also remember the Bible stories in Sunday school. The people there were nice and everything. Although, looking back, I don't seem to remember ever hearing about you must be born again and accept Jesus Christ into your heart.

Looking back now, I think that was probably the only real peace I had throughout the week. I thank God for being forced to go.

When I did go, and a lot of you can relate to this, parents would give you a quarter or fifty cents to put in your tithe envelope for the offering. I distinctly remember keeping that most of the time and just ripping it open and keeping the fifty cents. Oh, I was bad.

Nowadays, the children are not just keeping the money that is given them for Sunday school. What they are doing is going right in and taking their parents credit cards, running up hundreds or even thousands of dollars in bills, calling these crazy wild phone services and getting psychic readings performed for them.

Before, if we did something wrong, we would immediately be sat down, confronted and disciplined to a certain degree. We need to understand what the Bible says: **"Chasten thy son while there is still hope" (Proverbs 19:18).** My parents really truly believed and operated under the principle that a family needed discipline whenever and wherever it was necessary. The only thing was that there were times where I believe my father went out of control with that. But again, he did not know any better and did not know the Lord.

I want you to be encouraged and understand a key principle. The moment a parent allows their child to get over on them and not immediately confront them and bring the word and disciplines of correction, the parent has lost all respect from the child and lost the ability to correct and minister to them as a parent, something they should have at all times, and speak with that authority into their life. What I am really saying is that you have to love your child enough to tell them the truth, even if the old principle comes into play: "It's going to hurt me more than it hurts you."

Yes, it will hurt you to discipline your child even if the child cries back that they hate you in the temper of the moment, but understand and remember that you are helping right now to lay a foundation in their life so that when they grow old, according to the Bible, they will not depart from it. So parents, be encouraged and do the task at hand that you have been called to do.

> **LOVE YOUR CHILD ENOUGH**

# Chapter 3

## EATING FROM THE FORBIDDEN TREE

Growing up on the streets is not a lifestyle I recommend for anyone. One of the first things you learn growing up on the streets is to be a survivor. You learn to get street smart real fast. You are taught to get them before they get you. You're taught that when someone hits you, you hit them twice as hard to teach them a lesson so they do not come back again.

I want you to understand that the true message of this book is how to turn losing situations into victorious experiences in life, how to come out of the fast lane by making just one good solid responsible mature decision, and that decision is to accept Jesus Christ as your Lord and savior.

Let me turn the clock back until I was about eleven years old, getting tired of hearing my father come home drunk and screaming and yelling at my mother. I was getting blamed for everything and no one else in the family getting blamed at all, feeling like the black sheep of the family.

No matter what I did, I could not do anything right. And being that I was not getting the love and attention at home, I looked for it elsewhere. It's like an old song that used to be sung years ago, we are looking for love in all the wrong places. Well, that was me and that may have been you and a lot of others too. We went out there and we were looking for love. We really did not understand what we were looking for, we just wanted to be loved, feel wanted, needed, and accepted. We would try to get that love any way we could.

> **TURN LOSING SITUATIONS INTO VICTORY**

There are two kinds of fellowship in the world, the right fellowship and the wrong fellowship. If you are not getting your emotional needs fulfilled with the right fellowship, you will get them fulfilled with the wrong fellowship. That is exactly what happened to me.

At about eleven years old, you start feeling a lot of peer pressure. Understandably, the guys are starting to look at the girls in a different light. They are starting to think about dating, they are starting to get little crushes on people. The girls are starting to look at guys; they are starting to think about make-up and high heels, at eleven and twelve years old. The guys want to be popular with one another. No one wants to be the nerd or the outcast.

For me growing up with freckles, a little overweight, and all these strikes against me within my own mind, the peer pressure was just too much. So you want to be popular, and I wanted to be popular. What did I do? I just started hanging out with the wrong guys and doing the wrong things.

The first thing I started doing was drinking beer. You have to understand, drinking alcohol is sociably acceptable even today. Especially over thirty-five years ago, it was very much acceptable. I started drinking beer on a Friday and Saturday night. We would get someone to buy it for us and we would hide out and then sneak back home and cover our mouths and go right to bed and think that we were getting away with it.

But how many know that mothers, especially mothers, have what they call woman's intuition? They know if their child is doing something wrong, if they are lying, deceiving them, or just not acting right.

I encourage you mothers today to please listen to that inner voice inside of you and when it comes to your child, to love them enough to set them down and really get personal with them. Get involved in their lives.

Yes, go into their room, look through their room, look at their friends, and see who that person is that they are hanging around with. Love them enough to tell them that that person they are with is a creep and he or she is a manipulator and a liar, and will get them in trouble and refuse to let them go out with them. They might not like you for it now but later on, they will be very thankful for it. Now is the foundation time that you are setting for your child's life.

At eleven years old and twelve years old, I starting drinking and just trying to be accepted instead of being the outcast, I was still the odd one in the group. After drinking, the next step was smoking marijuana. Well, you know what happens when you drink alcohol and you smoke marijuana. You get high and you get what they call the munchies. You have an appetite, you want to eat and then you get tired and you just want to lay back, mellow out and sometimes take a nap.

Well that got old after a while. Pretty soon, an acquaintance, (someone that you know, because strangers do not walk up to you and offer you drugs) approached me and said,, "Jim, I have something here that will keep us awake so we don't have to fall asleep after we drink beer and smoke marijuana."

I said,, "What's that"? He said,, "It's called diet pills; they are speed pills. They are called white crosses and black beauties and robin eggs. You swallow a couple of these and they keep you awake , alert and going longer."

Well, of course I tried them. I wanted to be popular. I did not want to be the outcast and once I tried them, I enjoyed them. After a while, just a couple pills were not enough. Pretty soon, by fourteen years old, I was taking a handful of them. I was having a great time! I was popular with everybody, I had a good head on my shoulders (or so I thought), and I started buying and dealing large quantities of drugs early in life.

At fifteen years old, I got tired of taking the pills. They were getting to be really hectic on my nerves and I had another acquaintance say, "Jim, what you need to do is try this little bag of white powder." I asked, "What's that?" "They call it speed," he said,

> **NOW IS THE FOUNDATION TIME**

I said, "Well the pills I have, they call that speed." "Yeah, but this is a purer form of speed; it's called methamphetamine. What you need to do is snort this up your nose. One bag of speed is equal to about fifteen to twenty pills. It's a lot easier and you don't have to do all the pills and it doesn't work on your nerves as much."

Well, it sounded pretty logical to me, coming from an acquaintance, someone I knew, a supposed friend. So I tried this methamphetamine, this speed. And you know what? When I snorted it up my nose, it had a great burning sensation to it and it dripped in the back of my throat but I really enjoyed the effect of it. While I enjoyed the drug and alcohol, plain and simple, looking back, it only was giving me a temporary euphoria, an escape from reality. Reality for me was not very nice. So any escape was a relief.

I was not getting my emotions fulfilled in my family or in life. I continued on that path and lived my own separate life. My parents thought they knew me, but I really was not involved in the family life whatsoever.

My brother being two and a half years older than me was already into drinking alcohol and doing things on his own. My sisters were starting to come up into their teenage years. They were only two years behind me. I was getting well known as a drug dealer and the person to know.

Not only that, the drugs had another effect on me, they made me very angry at times and I became very physically abusive to individuals.

The abuse to other individuals as I look back now really started after I began snorting the methamphetamine.

About six months after learning how to snort methamphetamine that same "friend" came to me and said, there is another way to do get high that is a lot faster, easier, and would bring a better sense of euphoria. He told me the best way to do it was to inject it directly into my vein with a syringe.

At that point, I remember a fear coming over me and saying to myself that no, I should not do this. But because of the peer pressure and pride, I did not want to seem afraid to do something. So, of course, I said, that sounds like a great idea, let's do it. I allowed this individual to take this syringe and stick it into my arm and inject this methamphetamine directly into my vein and the effect was immediate and total euphoria, instant escape from reality.

It deadened all senses to the world and everything around me. It felt like heaven on earth. So of course, I fell right in love with this and I kept doing it for the next twenty years. I think this was the real deciding point and turning point in my life. It turned me into a person that was not only emotionally addicted to drugs but psychologically addicted as well. It took me to a point of no return.

Well, once you begin to get involved in this deeper type of drug abuse, you begin to get involved with deeper types of shady individuals in the wrong way. At sixteen years old with my altered driver's license, I began to get served in bars and liquor stores. I grew a mustache and went to liquor stores for alcohol and drugs, hung out at the wrong places with the wrong people, and began to really grow up fast. My teenage years quickly ended and I became an adult in my own mind at sixteen or seventeen years old.

One of the things that I am very thankful for is that my parents did insist that I finish high school. Even though I had problems in high school, like getting high and drinking alcohol by 8:00 am, in my last year, the school administration made it mandatory for me to participate in a special program where I would only be allowed in school from 8:00 am - 11:00 am, and then go to a job somewhere for the rest of the day.

> **I AM THANKFUL I FINISHED HIGH SCHOOL**

They did not want me in school all day causing problems. So I ended up getting a job at a local grocery store, a 7-11 type store at fifteen years old and actually managing the store by seventeen.

I began to take advantage of the authority that I had there and began to deal drugs directly from the store, acting like I owned the place.

When you get psychologically hooked on drugs you begin to get very prideful in what you are doing, you get to the point where you feel you really just do whatever you want. I became a very hard-hearted, very selfish individual, full of revenge.

Sooner or later, abuse of drugs and alcohol will lead you to two places: it will lead you to prison or to an early grave, or both. Well, thankfully, it had not led me to the grave. It came close at times, but it did eventually lead me to prison.

The first time I was arrested I was totally devastated. I had a lot of fear. But immediately, I was released on bail and I thought, well, this was not too bad.

Then I began getting involved with burglaries, stealing and being awake all night on methamphetamine (speed). On speed you don't sleep and you're doing just what the Bible talks about when it says *in John 3:19; "men loved darkness rather than light, because their deeds were evil"*. Evil deeds are done in darkness. I began to get involved with evil deeds, robberies, burglaries and selling drugs. I was doing things that were not anywhere close to being legal or moral.

Let me share with you some of the effects that drugs do have on an individual in your mind and in your personal life. I want you to remember this one thought: you can never satisfy the desires of the flesh. Your flesh will continue to crave more and more. It is only your soul that can be satisfied and only through Jesus Christ and His finished work at the Cross.

Let me share some truths with you right now. The main truth I want to tell you is this: drugs do give but they also take. And what they take is not worth what they give. If I were to write down all the things that drugs gave me, item by item, all of the good times, the fast money, the popularity, the sense of acceptance, the good feelings, the emotional highs, the adventurous

> **THE FLESH CAN NEVER BE SATISFIED**

experiences, I would probably be able to write a whole book about all the war-stories.

But also in the same retrospect, if I were to write down all the things that drugs took away from me mentally, physically, emotionally, socially and also spiritually, then we would probably have to write a series of books.

When someone begins to experiment with abusive drugs or alcohol, because nothing immediately happens, there is no immediate consequence, they fall into a false sense of reality and they really do not believe anything negative will ultimately happen.

Not only do drugs take away a lot from someone's life and soul, they also in fact give what people really do not want or need.

There are some real ultimate truths that go hand in hand in life with certain circumstances like if you eat too much sweets and candy, you eventually will have a lot of cavities. If you smoke a lot of cigarettes, you eventually end up with lung disease. If you eat a lot of the wrong foods, you will become obese and unhealthy and eventually end up on medications, in and out of hospitals and possibly having a shortened life and not living as long as God intended.

If something is true, you will either believe it or you will not believe it and have to prove it to yourself, the "hard way."

I wish that when I heard these things early in my life, I would have chosen to believe it. But I chose not to believe it, but ultimately, I did prove and to a large part I am still proving it today, that there are consequences to abusing drugs and alcohol.

Growing up, I started out drinking beer, which led to harder alcohol, then smoking reefer, taking pills and everything else. I really enjoyed the so called recreational drug use. It seemed that the drugs enhanced my mind. My senses of hearing, smelling, sight, and taste were sharpened and made everything I did more enjoyable. I really thought I could think better, sharper and clearer. It was almost like I could read minds. I could take in more, I could absorb more. I used to think, if I could just think, hear, and feel this way all the time, there wasn't anything I couldn't do.

I felt invincible, that this is the way life is supposed to be. But by the time I was entering into high school, I was failing and as I shared earlier, they did not want me in school, I was a trouble maker. It was not because I did not have a good mind to do the work, it's just that I did not want to or did not have the time to. I was too busy getting high and selling drugs. After about four to five years of doing different drugs fairly frequently, I found that my mind set really was not working so well later on in life; I could tell that I was thinking differently and slower. Because nothing immediately happened to me, I did not think anything would ultimately happen to me.

The very things that really sharpened my senses in the beginning were the very things that damaged my senses in the end.

Drugs put all your senses in overdrive, which eventually damages them. Even to this day, now I wear glasses, I do not see as well, I do not hear as well, I do not taste as well, and I definitely don't think as well, even though God has restored me to a certain degree in a lot of ways.

There were times I remember just thinking to myself, how did I get to this point? The point I was at was a point of no return. But while I was taking the drugs, I had a lot of energy. I could go and go and go. I could take drugs to stay awake, and take one to go to sleep. I could take a drug that would make me hungry and I would take one to quench my hunger.

With the drugs, I could control the natural workings of my whole life, including my body. But the drugs ultimately began to take from me in a physical sense. Because of taxing my body with not enough sleep, then too much sleep and not enough food, then too much food and not enough exercise, then too much exercise, my body began to break down so that my body would not respond naturally but only through the artificial means of using drugs.

Where my health at one time characterized my life, sickness began to characterize my life. I would really begin to facilitate from being real heavy to being real thin which took its toll on my heart and the inner parts of the body. Drugs altered me physically. Many years later I discovered that somewhere in the course of my drug use, I had become infected with hepatitis C.

From the social standpoint, what drugs did for me was that it allowed me to feel accepted, it gave me popularity, and it gave me a status quo. I had a lot of resources. When you have drugs and money, you have a lot of friends and you have an identity.

It also caused my personality to blossom. It gave me courage to be who I wanted to be and not what my parents said, I was going to be. It gave me the courage to do and say what I really wanted to do and say, but it did not stay that way.

What drugs ultimately took from me socially was really a total sense of rejection. I felt a total sense of rejection by my family, my friends and society. I felt isolated. I really did not want to be around anyone.

I felt like I needed to be by myself. I was very paranoid. I would switch vehicles every two weeks.

I became what we call today, a social outcast. Eventually, I ended up in total poverty. I ended up with nothing, in and out of prison.

Drugs are like an emotional elevator. They will stimulate your emotions to bring you up and just like you can reach those new heights, you will also reach new lows. It will bring you to a state of depression and sorrow; it will fill you with anger, hatred, jealousy, despair, greed, bitterness and unforgiveness. Because your emotions get artificially stimulated, they will cause you to go from extreme happiness to extreme depression, all within a couple hours' time span within one day and after a while, that has to take an effect and will damage your whole emotional make up to where it is hard for you to feel anything in a positive nature.

When you reach this point, the only way you can feel good at all is through drugs. Then you become not just physically addicted but you become psychologically and emotionally addicted as well, it feels like when you are on drugs, that's natural.

When my mother passed away, I felt no emotion. I felt a little sad but I really did not cry. It took thirteen months after my mother's death for me to break down to cry and sob from my heart. My own father had disowned me. He had written me off. He had threatened to divorce my mother if she continued to visit me while I was incarcerated. I even began to get drugs for my little sisters. I did not mean to do it but like a lot of things in my life, it just happened.

Because of drugs, my life was out of control and as a result, not only was I being destroyed, but everything in my path was also being destroyed. Yet I was blind to this fact. I thought I was helping people by selling them good drugs at a good price and even letting them have the drugs on a payment plan.

Oh yes, drugs gave to me emotionally, but it ultimately reduced me to an emotional state where the smallest little thing would set me off and in the wake of my emotional outbursts, I ended up in prison where I left a mother and a father to die without their son at their side.

> **MY LIFE WAS OUT OF CONTROL**

Space, time and the desire not to cause any more pain will not allow me to share concerning all of the lives I left damaged in the wake of my pursuing a good time. But even to this day, I just ask God to restore those individuals as he has restored me.

# Chapter Four

## THE FALL AND ITS CONSEQUENCES

Let me ask you a question: do you think any of the good times or the good feelings or the fast money or all of the nice material possessions were worth what it took from me and consequently took from others? Do you think for one moment that I could look back and say... yes, it was worth it?

Let me just share with you a few statements. I first started doing drugs to feel good, escape from reality, looking for love in all the wrong places. I ultimately did them just so I would not feel so bad.

I did them to awaken my emotions and I ultimately did them to numb my emotions.

I did drugs because they sharpened my senses, but ultimately they dulled and damaged my senses.

I did drugs because they made me more sociable, but ultimately they caused me to become isolated and anti-social.

I did drugs to become more loved and accepted and to feel wanted. Ultimately, I was rejected by everyone that I cared about.

I did drugs to have more friends, to have people around me all the time. But ultimately the drugs either killed my friends or landed them and me in prison where you really have no friends.

Initially, I did drugs to enjoy life. But ultimately, I did them in order to just get by in life.

Initially, I did drugs to improve my mind; ultimately drugs almost totally destroyed my mind.

Initially, I did drugs to fit in. Ultimately I was put into prison because I could not fit into society.

Initially, I did drugs to feel better about myself. Ultimately, I hated myself to the point that I wanted to commit suicide.

Initially I did drugs because I thought it would help me be all that I could be and wanted to be, but ultimately drugs caused me to be what I hated most in life, someone who was in prison, ashamed, and shaming my whole family.

Here is the lie that some of you or some of your children will tell themselves in order to adjust the truth that you just heard.... Well Jim, it happened to you because you lost control.

You did not know when to quit or when to stop. I'll be able to control what I do and how much I do. My only answer to that is Good Luck! Better men and women than you have tried. Besides, even if you are able to control it to a degree, you will suffer some sort of damage.

Drugs don't ever give to anyone without taking something from them. Trust me, ultimately what drugs have given you will not be worth what it takes from you. Now you can both learn and grow from it or you can ultimately do what I did for more than twenty years, learn the hard way and maybe end up in prison or lying in a casket somewhere with everyone looking over you. The choice is yours.

The best teacher is not experience; it is learning from the one who has walked through the personal experience. Please learn from my experience. Become a wise individual instead of what I was, a wise guy.

Eventually it got to the point where I just kept getting arrested, kept getting out on bail, getting an attorney, getting probation here and probation there, paying a fine here and paying a fine there. Then I ended up serving my first time in prison, six months.

Once I overcame the fear of going to prison, I started lifting weights and getting in shape, meeting new connections. I started that cycle of doing life on the installment plan.

You see, we all have certain fears that we live with and for someone that is involved with drugs and burglaries and illegal criminal activity, they have a fear of going to prison. But once you go the first time and overcome that fear, it's like the fear of using that needle for the first time. But the love of that drug over-rode the fear of the needle. Today we see the love of material possessions is also overriding the fear of God today.

I ended up with an arrest record, a rap sheet of 37 convictions, 20 felonies on my record. In 1981, I found myself having 62 warrants out for my arrest. I want you to know that you can run, but you cannot hide. Sooner or later, you get caught.

I got caught and I got placed inside the county prison and it took about five months to finally make bail and it was a bail that was not really proper.

I had someone that had some property and that already had liens upon it and got them to slip that property in front of the visiting judge and ended up making bail, going out and actually showing up for court the next day. They agreed to dismiss 45 charges if I plead guilty to 17.

So I plead guilty to 17 charges. Because I pled guilty, they allowed me to stay out on bail until the time of sentencing which was 45 days later.

About 40 days later, I received a letter in the mail stating that I was to be in court within five days for sentencing. I called my attorney up and I asked him what it looked like and how much time did he think I would get and he said, to me, "Jim you are going to go to prison for a few years." I thought to myself, well a few years isn't too bad.

That is how the mind gets. We think that going to jail for a few years is not bad at all. So I asked him how many years did he think I was going to receive. He said, he did not know exactly what I would get but said, I was facing 57 ½ to 115 years.

Well, I hung the phone up from my attorney and for the next five days all I could do was gather as many drugs and as much money as I could. I ripped people off, burned people for things and the day before it was time for me to go to court to get sentenced, I packed a bag, said goodbye to my family. My mother asked me, "When am I going to see you next?"

I said, "I will be in touch with you." I knew it broke her heart because I was going on the run. I was going to become a fugitive.

The next morning, I got on a train and went downtown Philadelphia to the Trailways Bus Station and I asked them, "What do you have going out of here this morning?"

They said,, "We have a bus going to Florida."

"That's not far enough," I said,.

They said,, "We have one that's going to Arizona."

**I KNEW IT BROKE HER HEART**

"Let me go there." I knew some people in Arizona.

So I got on the bus and as I am traveling on the bus, I began to speak with a young gentleman that was riding along with me and between Philadelphia and Pittsburgh. I got him high on drugs, smoking marijuana, snorting methamphetamine, taking pills and LSD. By the time he got off the bus in Pittsburgh, he was wasted, just a college student.

I continued to not only destroy my own life, but anyone that came in contact with me.

When the bus finally reached Arizona, I got off the bus, called the friends of mine, and they came down and picked me up. I explained the situation to them and they offered to let me stay at their house until I got on my feet, until I could afford to have my own place.

Well, I did go out there with another set of ID with the name of Robert Russ. I had acquired a little motorcycle and got a job at a pizza shop. So things were moving along pretty well for the first couple of months out in Arizona. I really did not change much, I was on the run.

Inside I was scared and I was reflecting back on my life and how I had arrived at this point of being on the run, with 62 warrants for my arrest, and facing 57 ½ to 115 years in prison.

The next thing I knew, I was lounging around the apartment out back by the pool and two gentlemen came walking up to me and said, hello and I said, hello. I said,, "Can I help you? I'm staying here with some friends." They said, "What's your name?"

I said, "Well, who are you?"

And he said, "I'm detective so and so and this is my partner."

At that point, my heart began to beat faster. "My name is Robert Russ."

"Do you have any identification?" he asked. I said, "what's this all about?' "I'm investigating something," he said,

"Sure, I have identification inside." I attempted to get up and go inside without the officers and they at one point put their hand on my shoulder and said, "We would like to go in with you."

I said, "That's not my apartment, I can't invite anyone in."

They said, "We know who you are Jim, we are here for you."

At that point, my eyes must have reflected the panic and they saw my reaction. I said, "I don't know what you are talking about. My name is Robert Russ." He said, "We want you to know we have the place surrounded. If you try to go out a window, you'll be captured."

So they took me into the police station and within 3 ½ hours after fingerprinting me, they identified who I was and placed me in Maricopa County Prison in Phoenix, AZ. Within a couple of weeks, they had me in front of the judge for extradition back to Pennsylvania.

I didn't fight extradition, and here's one reason why. The cells in that county prison were overcrowded and not many other inmates spoke English.

One day we were in the day room playing cards and watching television. The local news was on and they were reporting a story about a man who was arrested for murdering several people, cutting their bodies up and burying the body parts in the Arizona desert. I'm playing cards and looking at the news report. They showed a picture of the man who was arrested for these horrendous killings. I said to one of the other guys in the card game, hey, amigo, is that you on the television? He said no man, that's not me. I said, hey man that sure looks like you; maybe you got a twin brother? Amigo, are you sure that's not you? He then got this crazy look in his eye and yelled in my face, look man, that's not me! I said, okay, okay man, that's not you.

Now you know one reason I didn't fight extradition, would you?
So I was extradited back to Pennsylvania and I stood in front of the sentencing judge. He began to tell me what a menace to society I was, how I should not be allowed on the street for a long period of time, how arrogant I was and then he proceeded to sentence me to 8 ½ to 17 years in the State Penitentiary. And then away I went to prison for a long, long time.

I remember sitting in my cell that night, with thoughts of suicide and reflecting back on my life. I remember thinking how rotten I was, and how terrible I was. I thought about the time when I actually put a woman in my car trunk because she talked too much. How I stopped the car, wrapped her in wire I ripped out from under the dashboard of the vehicle, locked her in the trunk, and finally let her out miles down the road behind a 7-11 store.

I remember stabbing someone where it took seventy-six stitches to sew them back together because he owed me money. He only owed me about $40.00. I beat people with sticks and baseball bats and stabbed them with knives. I just ruined people's lives and shamed my family day after day, week after week in the town we had lived.

I remember thinking to myself that I just ruined my whole life and everyone else's life. It was time to take my own life here in this prison cell and just put an end to the misery, not only in my own life but the misery I caused in anyone that has come in contact with me.

# Chapter 5

## THE WILDERNESS YEARS

During the eleven years that I spent in Pennsylvania prisons, the challenge of survival kept me plodding through the darkness of life. There I sat with an eight and a half to seventeen year prison sentence, with thoughts of suicide running through my head, watching all the TV movies and shows about jail or prison that never came close to capturing the intense trauma and drama that occurs when that steel door slams shut behind you.

I went from money in my pocket, new rental cars every two weeks, lots of drugs, plenty of laughter, fun and parties, to sitting in a lonely prison cell. No more good and fancy times. I was suddenly jammed in with thousands of other men. I was just another statistic. I was lonely. Deep inside, I was scared, I was hurting and I wanted to die.

But something deep within me kept me going. I don't know if it was God just pressing me forward, I don't know if it was my pride, or whatever it was, but I did not commit suicide. Here I was, behind the wall at Graterford State Penitentiary, 4,000 men, one of the most notorious prisons in the state of Pennsylvania, known for its stabbings, rapes, hard times and all the tough guys that were sent there. Deep inside, I never thought of myself as a tough guy. I was that scared little boy worrying about my father coming home and hitting me for what I had done.

I was placed on a cell block with a 1,000 other men, 60% black, 25% white, 15% Spanish. I needed to re-evaluate my life; I needed a new game plan. The old timers had some solid advice, "Serve your time one day at a time, watch your back and be careful who you talk to. Don't owe anyone any money, do not borrow off of anyone, keep a low profile." No problem I thought, I'll just hang in there and be cool. Do my time, learn whatever I can and try to make it out of here, but it seemed like a lifetime. It seemed like my life was over.

For the next few months while I was being classified, I took an evaluation of my life. I met one individual there, he was a pretty tall fellow 6'3," 220-some pounds, pretty well built and we had become friends and we talked about doing our time together. He had given me some insight on how to get to a certain institution.

You place down names saying you had enemies in other state prisons and you could not go to those places.

So a few months later, I was being placed on a bus and transferred to State Correctional Institute of Camp Hill, PA.

As I settled into the prison routine, I began to listen to the old timers and watching how they handled situations and began to befriend a few other people. I want you to understand that doing time is not easy. Oh, anyone can do time, in fact, the only thing some people can do is time. But to survive the long calendar and not become just another old timer, that's the real battle. I began to gather all the information and ideas I could from the older cons who were inside and began to figure how to stay alive and to develop my own plan of action.

Well, what I decided was that I was going to take advantage of this time and I would hang up my life of crime in dealing drugs and that I would take advantage of all the educational opportunities and go to college while I was in there, better myself and when I got out, I would stay out. I would live life in society, the way that society expected me to.

So I figured step one was to stay in good physical shape and start lifting weights and jogging. So every morning, I hit the physical exercise yard, lifted weights, jogged, played handball and basketball. I figured my next step would be to take care of my mind set so I began to sign up for some programs to get involved in.

I found out something: the prison system is so overcrowded that when I signed up for programs, I sat down with them and they told me I had too much time. I would not be allowed to participate in the programs yet. I asked them why? They said because the other inmates that were closer to being

> **TAKE ADVANTAGE OF THIS TIME**

released, those within two to three years of their parole date, they get first choice in the programs.

So I had an eight and a half year minimum, so I would have to wait five to six years before I would be allowed in any program. I asked them, what am I supposed to do for the next five to six years and this is what they told me. They said, "We don't care what you do; just don't give us a hard time."

Well, you have to understand, I was in there for being rebellious and not listening to authority and when they began to speak to me with that type of attitude, this brought up a rebellious spirit within me.

I went back and had to devise a new plan. How am I going to do this time the best way?

Well, let me share something with you. When you are serving a long sentence, you want to be as comfortable as possible and to be as comfortable as possible inside a prison, you need money and in order to have money, you either need to have people on the outside that are going to send you as much money as you need or you are going to have to make that money yourself.

In prison, you don't make a whole lot of money. You start out at about 15 cents an hour and you can go as high as 45 cents an hour which would give you approximately anywhere from $12-15 a month to $50 a month and that's not a whole lot of money to survive real comfortable inside a prison.

Then there is the other way, and that way is to do the same thing you were doing on the street, acquire lots of money illegally. I began to devise a plan of action to deal drugs inside the institution with other individuals, getting drugs sent inside and began to have black market stores and sell football pool tickets, etc. I became quite good at it. After a while, I was keeping about $1,000 cash stashed inside the institution.

I had guys on every block dealing drugs and I began to just acquire a lot of comforts. The comforts I did acquire were pretty amazing. I had wall-to-wall carpet in my cell, a color TV, a nice stereo system, a 12 cup coffee pot, a hot plate, where I could have filet mignon, steak and eggs, breakfast, lunch and dinner if I wanted it.

We were selling a lot of marijuana. There were times we went through a pound of marijuana every month or two. We were making lots of money in there. When I say we, I mean the cohorts that I was involved with. You never do anything on your own inside a prison. You always have someone associated with you and you have to be careful who you associated with so you could continue your illegal activity.

It got to the point where we even had kittens for pets on each block. I had a little kitten and nicknamed her Gremlin, after the movie, The Gremlins.

I captured the wild kitten at the furniture factory and brought it to my cell. Its eyes were infected and because the little kitten looked so weird, the nickname stuck. One of the nurses had given me some medication for the cat's eyes and it became healed! This cat eventually had two litters of kittens under my bed.

I kept Gremlin for about two years in my cell before the authorities said; I'd have to get rid of her.

You have to understand something; there are no totally straight institutions. There is always some illegal activity going on and there is always a price to buy "something" or "someone." If you can be bought, the devil will pay the price.

For quite a long time inside the institution, the guards allowed inmates to help them run the blocks as we helped keep things calmed down. It's a shame, but you have two to four officers on a cell block with 200-1,000 inmates. These men are to control the block and the correctional officers do have a tough job to do and I would not want to be in their position.

Another thing that became a great escape was reading a lot of books and keeping your brain from getting rusty and dusty, many of the men around me were sinking, giving up, falling apart. They were shutting themselves down by just closing off the world and incarcerating themselves behind metal walls. I'd see them sitting in their cells staring at the floor, doing nothing but time. Instead of taking advantage of the time, they would let time do them in. They would not read or write or participate in any of the programs. The time and wait of incarceration was doing them in. Without even realizing it, they decided to die on the installment plan because life had lost all of its value to them.

> **IF YOU CAN BE BOUGHT, THE DEVIL WILL PAY THE PRICE**

I made up my mind; this was not going to happen to me. I tried to stay active in a lot of different things. Letter writing and involvement in positive activities, interaction in communication with other people were important aspects in my plan.

My plan was very simple right from the beginning. When you go to prison, everyone has a certain amount of fears they live with and they all want to hook up with someone. So I hooked up with key individuals, one in particular was Joe, whose nickname was "Josie Wales." What a fellow this guy was. He is still incarcerated, still doing time. He was what he called an outlaw that would never die. I liked him, he was committed, he was loyal and he was faithful.

One thing I want to share with you is that people in prison, they have a loyalty; there is a bond you'll never understand unless you do time with an individual. Being from the old school, you just don't turn or rat on your friends.

You hang in there, you stay faithful to them, and you commit to them. Even after I became born again, I never deserted the people I hung around with in the prison.

I am still there for them today, to love them, to encourage them and to do whatever I can for them without involving any sinful ways.

People would look at me and wonder, how do you do it, how are you surviving? How are you just hanging in there? But deep down inside my heart and my soul, I was experiencing the same war that everyone else was. Something was missing. There would be times late at night where I would just pace back and forth without hope. I would be getting high just to try to bury that feeling of hopelessness.

What happened was that I really got caught up into a false sense of reality, living behind a mask of fear, loneliness, despair and hopelessness. Day after day, I would be doing the same old things, the same old, same old, as they call it. The question that kept running through my mind was what am I doing here? I don't fit the profile of the average prisoner. Most prisoners have a sixth grade education. In eighth grade, I had an IQ of 129. I graduated high school. What happened? Where did I go wrong?

> **I WAS A PRODUCT OF MY OWN CHOICES**

Then it dawned on me one day that I was a product of my own choices. That's right. Decisions that I had made put me where I was. Life was not a matter of chance, life was a matter of choice, but I still was not ready to change my life. I still continued just selling drugs and getting high and doing what I wanted to do even in prison.

I remember one day, I was working in the furniture factory, and word came through that the "goon squad" (security team) was on their way for me. I began to run through the furniture factory getting rid of my football tickets, the money in my pocket and the drugs in my pocket. I ended up in the front by the office. The correctional officers there took me and threw me up against the wall and said, "You are under arrest." I said, "You can't arrest me, you are nothing but a rent-a-cop, you are not a real cop. I've been under arrest for the last five years."

That did it, that got them mad and they threw the cuffs on me, they yanked my arms up from behind me and away I went to what is called the hole (solitary confinement). They call it Mohawk in Camp Hill State Prison. They threw me into a cell and gave me my write-ups (disciplinary actions).

On the write-ups I was charged with inciting a riot, attempted homicide because I had chased someone down and stabbed them with a broken part of a nail clipper. I remember getting put into the hole for 180 days, six months.

The hole is a five by seven cell where you only came out twice a week for forty-five minutes for a short period of exercise and a short shower, then back in your cell you went. The cells are set up side by side and you never get to see the person next to you. You talk to other inmates in the hole, but it's really not talking, it's loud noise, shouting and screaming all day and night. All you could do in there was read. But let me tell you, even in the hole we got drugs and extra food delivered.

One thing I remember about serving time in prison, there was no peace in there. There is absolutely no peace whatsoever. You never got a moment to yourself. It was total chaos!

When I got released from the hole, I went back out to population and got involved in my illegal activity once again. My home boys would be there waiting to get me started by supplying me with drugs, and that's how we looked out for one another.

> **THERE IS NO PEACE IN PRISON**

## Chapter 6

### FEAR OF DEATH

One of the biggest fears everyone has when they get sentenced to a long period of time in prison is that a loved one will die while they are incarcerated: a mother, a father, a grandfather, a special aunt or uncle, a spouse, a child. That fear just hangs over you like a dark cloud, day after day. The sense of helplessness that you cannot do anything or just be there with your loved ones is something that each and every inmate lives with day in and day out.

No matter how big, bad and tough inmates think they are, they are like a little child when this fear looms over them every day of their incarceration period. Well, this fear hung over me also.

> **FEAR HANGS OVER YOU**

I did not get many visits while I was there, maybe once or twice a year, my mother would come up and my sisters might come up with her and I really valued those times and I look back and thank God for Moms.

Mothers hang in there with you no matter what you have done, no matter how many times you go to jail or what you are charged with, they still love you. They have an unconditional no-strings-attached love for you. My Dad on the other hand wrote me off a long time ago, even threatened to divorce my mother if she kept coming to visit with me.

My brother and I were never close, but my sisters, I would occasionally telephone them. My sister, Debbie had gotten what they called born again, saved, and she kept telling me I needed Jesus. I said, that's good for you but that's not for me.

One day I got a message that I needed to go up to my counselor's office, who was Mr. Jeff Ditty, and call home. I left my cell thinking, what could this be all about? Once I got to my counselor's office, he informed me that I needed to call home, that my mother needed to speak to me. Talking with my mother, she told me she had to go into the hospital and get an operation because of her diabetes. She went from 300 pounds to about 150 pounds after she found out she had diabetes. She had lost a lot of weight and she began to shrink.

She asked me to pray for her and she wanted to explain all of this before she went into the operation because you never know what can happen when you go in for surgery. They were going to have to amputate her left leg up to her knee.

I remember going back to my cell that day and talking to God. I did not really know God at that time in my life, but I remember saying, "God, why are you letting this happen to my mother? What kind of God are you to let this happen to this woman who never hurt anyone, who took this abuse from my father all her life and how I shamed her as son? Why are you letting this happen? But I also remember saying to Him, "God, please don't let anything happen to her during this operation. Don't let her die; let her live through it."

After she had the operation, I called home and talked to my sisters and brother and they told me she lived through the operation. I don't remember if I ever thanked God for answering that prayer or not because I did not really know God.

A few months later, my brother brought mom up to visit me. I was all excited that day to just see her. My emotions were running high, hugging her, crying and sobbing. Maybe part of it was that I was looking at her walking with a cane due to the fact that she had one of these prosthetic legs now. When the visit was over, I remember walking back from the visiting room to my cell thinking to myself, who was that woman?

The woman I just had a visit with was not like the mother I was used to. You see, my mother used to be happy and jolly. A fun type of woman, nothing ever got her down. She enjoyed life no matter what was going on. But this woman I just had a visit with was different. She did not feel like a complete woman anymore, missing a part of her body. She did not feel like a complete mother, a complete wife. She had lost her zest for life. She had lost that happy-go-lucky way about her. She was pale, white, and walking slow and there was something so different about this woman. It just did not remind me of my mother.

After being in prison now for about four years, the outside world was changing, but I was not. I was still the same individual who was selfish and hard-hearted. My goodness, what was going on? What was happening? It seemed like the world was changing outside but my time was standing still. I remember thinking to myself as I cried myself to sleep that night, who am I? Well, even though life was changing on the outside, I continued in my daily routine.

I remember going right back to my drugs and stash and getting high that night. My heart was still hard and calloused.

My sister kept telling me I needed the Lord and that she and her husband were praying for me, but I did not want to hear it. I continued to use and deal drugs.

During the course of that next year, a friend of mine, who was dealing drugs in the prison for me and was serving a life sentence, became born again. His story is that at seventeen years old, he with another person, went into an establishment to rob it and did not realize someone was in there. The other individual took the life of that person, not him, but he was there. He ended up pleading guilty by association, and at seventeen years old, for the crime of second degree murder, he was sentenced to life in prison.

He had become born again which I did not know. One day I went down to his cell and said, "Hey man, here's your drugs to deal." He had taken the package and looked at me funny. Later on he told me he had given that package to somebody else to sell. He brought me the money and said, "Jim, I don't want any drugs any more, I am now born again and I am walking with Jesus." I thought to myself, you'll be back. He said, "I love you in the Lord and I am going to pray for you." I said, "Sure, that's great, you do that."

It was during the next twelve months of my life that I was allowed to finally begin to sign up for some programs. One of the programs that I signed up for was a two year computer class. I remember signing up for the class and being called over to the school and given a test.

After the test, I got called back over and sat down with the teacher and he explained to me that I had passed the test and that he wanted me to enter into the program, but that the security staff of the institution came to him and they were very concerned about me having access to any computers because of the illegal activity that I was doing inside the institution, that the staff was concerned I would use the computers to print up football pool tickets and for other illegal activities.

> **I LOVE YOU IN THE LORD AND I AM GOING TO PRAY FOR YOU**

The teacher of this class said, to me that he spoke up for me and that he wanted me to have the same opportunity to get an education as anyone else and that he was going to take a chance and allow me to enter into the class. I remember thinking, "Wow, here is someone who is giving me a second chance, wasn't that wonderful.

Why would he do this for me? He does not even know me. He stood up to the security office for me to get an education."

Even today, I still have a lot of respect for this individual who would do something like that for me, for someone he really did not know. He knew of my reputation, but he still took a chance with me.

Looking back, this teacher was hearing from God. The Holy Spirit was "even now" starting to put my new life together. Equipping me for the ministry He had for my life.

I entered into this computer class and right after I started this class, within a couple months, I had received a message from one of the correctional officers on the block that my counselor wanted to see me. He informed me that I was to go immediately to my counselor's office. When I got there, he told me I was to call home, there was an emergency situation.

I had called home and my brother said, to me that my mother had a massive heart attack the night before. She was sitting home watching the television show called "Cheers." Mom laughed so hard watching the actress Rhea Perlman, who played the woman Carla, that she had a massive heart attack. She was rushed to the hospital. I asked my brother what hospital she was in. He said she is not in the hospital. She was in the morgue. The heart attacked had killed her.

I remember getting quiet and hanging up the phone. My counselor looked at me asking what was wrong. I said; my mother died. I remember walking slowly back to my prison cell and going in there and just sitting there thinking about it. I don't remember crying. I remember being sad, lonely, feeling the loss, but I don't remember crying. My heart had gotten that hard. My conscience had become that seared.

The only way for someone that is serving time to be allowed out to a funeral is to go back in front of the judge. Your family has to go back in front of the judge and pay an attorney, fees, and pay the sheriff's department to transfer you to the funeral and my family did that. It cost them about $1,500.

I was transferred from the State Correctional Institute of Camp Hill to State Correctional Institute of Graterford which was close to my family's home. I remember them taking me out to the funeral parlor in a van with cuffs and shackles around my legs, feet, wrists, and waist.

When we arrived at the funeral parlor, they slid open the side of the sheriff's van and they said, "Ok, come on lets go."

I said, "Well take these cuffs and shackles off."

They said, "Oh no, you ran before, we're not taking them off of you." I said, "I can't go in and pay my last respects to my mother like this. I would not disrespect her and ruin her funeral like this."

He said, "We don't trust you." I said, "Then I am not going in."

I remember my father and my brother coming out to the Sheriff's van, this was the first time in over five years I had seen and spoken to my father because he had disowned me when I went to prison. I remember him saying to me, "Son, it's ok, she'll understand." So I got out of the van with the shackles around my feet, the waistband and handcuffs, holding my hands close to my waist where I could not move them, walking slowly step by step into the funeral parlor. It was before the actual service time. I was told I would get fifteen minutes, not a minute more.

So I slowly walked up to the casket and looked in. As I looked to my left, there was a sheriff's deputy standing at the head of my Mom's casket and as I looked to my right, there was another one standing at her feet. This is how I had to pay my last respects to my mother, surrounded by armed sheriffs and in cuffs and shackles.

I felt at that time like a low life disrespectful shamed son, in that this is how I had to say goodbye to my mother. I remember bowing my head and going down on my knees and saying goodbye to Mom. Then standing up, walking over to my sisters, my father and brother. I could not hug them because of the amount of handcuffs and shackles with which I was bound.

So they hugged me, said goodbye. My father said goodbye son. It was the first time in many years that my father had called me son. At that point, my heart began to sink and emotions began to well up inside of me, not over my mother's death but over the fact that my father had called me his son.

For years, it seemed he would pronounce curses over my life. Statements like, telling me you are not my son, we brought the wrong child home from the hospital, and you'll never amount to anything.

> **MY FATHER CALLED ME SON**

37

You're rotten, no good and that someday you will end up in prison.

But at that moment, something within me grabbed a hold of the fact that he called me his son. I was taken back to the prison van and whisked away back to Graterford prison, and then transferred back to the Camp Hill prison. Immediately when I got back to Camp Hill, I went right to my drug stash and got high again.

## Chapter Seven

### MY BURNING BUSH EXPERIENCE

Over the next few months I began to sink deeper into a state of depression, loneliness and despair. My heart had become even harder and my conscience more seared. What would it take for me to wake up to reality?

For the next year, I just began to live life as a zombie day in and day out. Oh yes, I attended computer classes. I began to get more involved in handball, lifting weights and running more miles. I was beginning to get in good physical shape. I was down to about 170 pounds and that was quite a change because I was up over 235 pounds at one time. Physically I was doing okay. Mentally, I felt my mind was pretty sharp. I was on top of the prison world, wheeling and dealing. I was the business man; I was the top drug dealer in the prison at that time. Even though I was on top, I was really hitting the bottom of the heap, so to speak.

About thirteen months after my mother's death the correctional officer once again said to me that my counselor, Jeff Ditty wanted to see me and that I needed to go to his office. I responded, "Look, I don't want to go see this man; every time I see him, he has nothing but bad news for me."

> **I WAS REALLY HITTING BOTTOM**

I remembered going to see him when my mother was in the hospital getting her leg amputated, asking him if I could call the hospital and talk to her. I tried to call the hospital and there was a miscommunication on the phone. I finally got through but he was telling me my time was up and that I needed to hang up. I got into an argument with him, wanting to go across the desk at him, grab him by the neck and punch him. He told me to get out of his office and go back to my cellblock.

I returned to my cell and started packing up my belongings; I figured the counselor was going to have me sent to the hole for threatening him, because that is what they did when they were threatened.

Sure enough, the guard came to my cell and informed me that Mr. Ditty told him to just keep me in for the day that I needed to calm down because my mother was in the hospital and said, it's understandable that my actions were undesirable.

I thought, boy, what a softie he is! It was this same counselor that called me up to his office to call home when my mother died and I remembered that he showed me compassion, that he was very kind and gentle that day.

It was this same counselor that wanted to see me again, and I thought, oh man, here we go again. I told the officer on the block to tell him I didn't want to see him. Then, the guard gave me a direct order to go see him. To disobey him meant I would be thrown into the hole. So I gave in went up to see him.

I sat down across from him at his desk and asked him what he wanted. He said, "Well, I just wanted to see how you were doing, Jim. I was going over your file and seeing that you are now involved in computer classes and I felt compelled to call you up to talk to you."

He asked me if there was anything he could do for me. I said, "Yes, I would like to transfer to another institution. I am tired of being here. I would like a change." He said, "We can't just transfer you at a whim." I said, "Could I get a different job, could I do something else?" He said, "No, you need to stay where you're at." I asked him a few more things and he said,, not right now. I said, "What about furloughs?" (Furloughs are a pass to go home.) He said, "Not yet, you don't have enough time in for that."

We went back and forth for a few minutes, me telling him what I wanted and him telling me no. Finally, this man looked directly into my eyes and said, "Jim, what is going on in your life? What's really wrong?" I looked at him and I just blurted out "I miss my mother." I put my head in my hands and began to cry and sob like a baby. Finally after thirteen months since she died, I wept over the death and loss of my mother.

**I MISS MY MOTHER**

This man sat there in silence and he let me cry. He handed me some tissues and finally when I was done, I composed myself and got myself back together somewhat, he leaned over and opened up one of his drawers in his desk and he pulled out a Bible. I thought to myself, Oh no, he is going to preach to me.

You see, I had heard some rumors about this man. I heard he was one of those born again Jesus freaks. Immediately my wall went up. I sat there thinking to myself; be careful Jim, watch out that he does not get to you. So this man said, to me "Jim, I want to talk to you a few minutes about God." He said, "Jim, do you believe in God?" "Of course I do, doesn't everyone?" Then he asked "Jim, do you believe in Jesus Christ, that he is real?" I said, "Yes. I believe in Jesus Christ." I thought to myself, let me just trick him, let me stop him now before he goes any further.

So I said, to him "Wait a minute, before you go any further with this, let me share with you that I understand what you are trying to say to me and I want you to know that I'm a Christian."

He said, "Oh really? Why do you say that you are a Christian?"

I said, "I believe in God and Jesus Christ. Growing up, I went to church every week and Sunday school and I still go to church now."

"Oh, do you really? How often is that?" He asked.

I said, "Well I go occasionally on Sunday's but I go at least twice a year. I make sure I go at Christmas to celebrate Jesus' birth and I go at Easter and celebrate His resurrection on the cross. So I'm a Christian."

He said to me, "Jim that is not what makes you a Christian." I got mad because I felt he was coming against me and totally not believing me and calling me a liar.

So I blurted out to him "Well, yeah, then you tell me what makes a Christian?" He said, "I'm glad you asked."

This person, this godly man full of the love of God, for the next hour, proceeded to explain to me what makes a Christian. For the next hour, all he did was share with me who God the Father is, who God the Son is, and who God the Holy Spirit is. He told me about the love of Father God, the love of Jesus Christ and the love of the Holy Spirit.

He very simply explained to me what Jesus Christ did on the Cross at Calvary. He explained everything

**WHAT MAKES A CHRISTIAN?**

to me in very simple ways of what God did for me and for the world and not once did this man ever point out my sin, the things that I was doing wrong. He never pointed out my drug dealing and my illegal black market stores. Not once in that whole hour do I remember him pointing his finger at me or once pointing out my sin. All he did was share with me the love of God and what God has done for me.

He explained to me what the term "born again" really means. Then he quietly asked me one question. "Jim, give me one good reason . . . You've tried everything else; why won't you try God's way?"

I left his office and went back to my prison cell. Quietly, I pulled the sheets off my bed and hung them over the cell bars.

I didn't want anyone to see what I was about to do. I got down on my knees, and then I talked to God, and asked Him a lot of questions.

All questions from my heart. "God, where's my mother? Is she with you? Is she in purgatory? God, I miss my mother! I don't know if you're real or not. I just can't stand this pain, living with this pain every single day since my mom died. God, I miss my mother! I don't know where she's at." I sobbed uncontrollably as I continued, "God, I have tried everything else. Jesus, I don't know if your blood flowing from the cross can forgive all of my sins, because I've been a dirty dog. But, if you can, forgive me, please do it, Jesus. I can't live with this pain anymore. Show me you're real. Take over my life God!"

After fifteen minutes of crying and sobbing, I got up and washed my face real quick. I wanted to make sure nobody saw the tough guy bawling like a little kid. I stood in front of my window, staring outside.

As I stood there, it dawned on me. For the first time in thirteen months since mom died, I had peace. The pain was gone! "Wait a minute," I thought. "I asked God to take away my pain . . . and he did."

> **I GOT DOWN ON MY KNEES AND TALKED TO GOD**

In a flash, I was at my cell door. "Hey, I want to go back and talk to that counselor!" "Well," the Correctional Officer hesitated, "You don't have a pass." "Look," I argued, "He's always calling to see me, now I need to see him!"

So I was permitted to go see him. I explained to him what I did and what happened. He said, to me, "You got born again, Jim, that's great!" He gave me a Bible and told me to start reading it.

Immediately, I destroyed hundreds of dollars of drugs by flushing them down the toilet, wiped all my debts clean, and closed all of my black market stores. The prison drug supply dried up and inmates were upset. "Snap out of this religious thing," they'd complain. "We need drugs!" "It's not a religious thing," I'd reply.

So I was now on fire for God. When you're on fire for God, you can't just sit still. You want to grow, you want to learn, and you want to be held accountable. To fan these flames, you need someone with more wisdom, understanding, and knowledge than yourself; you need a teacher.

So one day, I asked another Christian inmate, "That pastor that comes in to see you, can I write to him?" He gave me the address, so I wrote to him, telling him I wanted to be discipled.

## Chapter Eight

### GOD'S PATRIARCHS

After waiting a couple of months, a local church where the Senior Pastor, Larry Titus at that time, who had a heart for prison ministry, asked one of his associate pastors to go to the prison and to disciple me within the prisons visiting room. This man of God, Pastor Steve Boyer, would come in faithfully week after week, teaching me the Word of God. I would come out to the visiting room with lists of questions about what I was reading and I wanted to know the truth and correct way to apply the Word in my own life. He and his wife Carla, received me into their home when I was released from prison and showed me an example of what a Christian home should be.

Then after I was released, I had the opportunity to sit at the feet of another man of God, brother John Anwyll, who has studied the different versions of the Bible and taught me from the best word to word translation there is, the King James version, which I still use to this day. Because of his teaching, I have held true to the Word of God all of these years.

The Lord continues to put Godly men of the Word in my life to disciple me in truth. I've been extremely blessed to be mentored and taught by some of the best teachers in the body of Christ. I'll be eternally grateful to Jeff Ditty, Pastor Larry Titus, Pastor Steve Boyer., Pastor Dave Hess., Pastor Dave Landis, Pastor Jack Cashman, and Pastor David Borg.

Two months later, I was reading books by Kenneth Copeland and Kenneth Hagin about the baptism of the Holy Spirit. I was in my cell, reading away, and as I turned the pages, my stomach started to rumble. My eyes continue to drink in the words on the Holy Spirit baptism. As I turned another page, waiting for my eyes to finish its words, my stomach thundered inside. "Am I hungry," I wondered? "Wait a minute, I just ate!"

All of a sudden, it hit me. BOOM! It was like countless light bulbs had gone off in my cell! I couldn't see anything but bright light. "Whoa, what did I eat for lunch?

"What's going on here?" I thought. So I called to my Christian friend in the cell below. "Yo, Denny put your

> **IT HIT ME BOOM!**

mirror out and look up here! Does it look real bright in my room?" He carefully stretched his mirror out with his skeptical face peering up.

"Hey," he asked, "did you backslide already? Are you smoking pot? Give me some!"

"I'm not backsliding," I yelled back. "I'm reading these books on the baptism of the Holy Ghost."

"Oh, man," he said,, "you're in for it now. You've been baptized in the Holy Spirit! That's better than getting high." It sure was, my heart was blazing. I was really on fire for God!

My life has never been the same since the infilling of the Holy Spirit. I would encourage each and every believer to seek the infilling for themselves.

# Chapter Nine

## MINISTRY BEGINS AND THE RIOT ERUPTS

After I got born again and filled with the Spirit, I went from being the top drug dealer to the top soul winner. Each morning, as soon as my cell door opened, I headed out with my bible tucked under my arm. People would duck and weave to get away, avoiding me like a thunderous storm. But I didn't care. There were souls to save!

I started holding Bible studies out in the prison yard. My first ministry was to those who were on Thorazine. They were the "B-block inmates," the guys who had mental challenges in their lives. Nobody messed with them. But God put compassion in my heart for them. In the prison yard, I would gather them around me to have a Bible study.

> **BORN AGAIN AND FILLED WITH THE SPIRIT**

I want to tell you about this. One guy, "Amtrak," he had been run over by a train. Guys would come over to the study and yell at him, "Hey, Amtrak, why don't you come over here and shine my shoes?" I would jump to my feet and say, "Look, man, I'm not that saved yet, back off or I'll backslide for five minutes. Now you leave Amtrak alone!"

"All right," they'd shrink back. "Okay, Jim, it's all right." But it wasn't all right. I wouldn't let them bust on him anymore. "He's not just Amtrak," I'd spout. "That's brother Amtrak to you!"

I wasn't saved that long or sanctified much yet, but the only church model I knew was the book of Acts. You have faith, you believe, trust in God, and God will provide. Sometimes, He won't do it how you expect Him to, but God always comes through. He knows what you need. And He cares about everything.

When you go about doing what the Lord wills, He will make sure you're taken care of. Even with the little things. Things like the weather for a Bible study held outside in the prison yard. Sometimes I'd wake up to rain pouring down like sheets outside. But, I'd still go out for a Bible study in the rain. I'd just ask God, "God, please stop the rain. I need an hour and a half." The rain would stop and as soon as the Bible study was over, it would begin to rain again. Meanwhile, the seeds had been planted. All I did was obey and plant, then God would provide the water to nourish them. People would get saved, healed, and delivered off their medications.

Some would get back on their medications. But, I would just continue to love them and share the Gospel with everyone, just like Jesus wanted us to. The only true church I have ever known is the book of Acts, even to this day. This is how I live my life.

Not long after my encounter with Christ, my faith was put to the test. On October 25, 1989, the Camp Hill riots hit. It lasted over four days and three nights, with 16 buildings destroyed and more $35,000,000 dollars' worth of damage as inmates took over the prison.

**THE SEEDS WERE PLANTED**

At the time, I had just moved into a modular unit. (Mobile homes used in prisons to house inmates.) Our guard was a Christian man. We would fellowship with him and he would treat us right.

Ninety-five percent of your inmates just want to do their time and go home. Ninety-five percent of your correctional officers just want to do their job and go home. But, there's five percent on both sides that are greedy, power-hungry, and full of pride. Thankfully, this Officer was one of the praiseworthy ones. He always took care of us, treated us with respect. So, when those riots hit, we returned his actions of loving-kindness and took care of him.

Immediately, the Officer locked himself in his office cubicle per institutional policy. Meanwhile, my fellow inmates and I barricaded the doors and windows. In the midst of the riot, the voices of outside rebels would call to us, "Hey Jim, just let us have the guard. . ." Gushing from their voices, their waves of pure hatred emanated through the door. "No way," we'd yell back. Then they would try to climb in the window, we'd smack their hands with a broom. "Stay out of here man, you can't come in here or have this guard, we're protecting him, go about your business elsewhere."

It wasn't long, though, before they returned with more hostile ambitions. Black clouds of smoke smoldered around the compound. The storm of rebellion was now heating up with spiteful passion. Before long, we started to smell smoke close to our unit. They were trying to set our unit on fire with us in it. But check this out, it wouldn't burn! God showed me in the spirit that he had angels blowing out the flames as they were lit. Most of the other modular units burned down; ours didn't. It simply wouldn't burn down. So, the stubborn rebels resorted to more force. They had crowbars and tried to pry open our doors and windows. But I believe the angels of God surrounded us, holding those flimsy boards strong.

The riots worsened. We couldn't keep the Officer safe forever. He needed to get out. So, several of the brothers and I went to his office. "We need you to trust us. "We have to get you out of here." We gave him an inmate's uniform. "We want you to put these clothes on, take the battery out of your walkie-talkie to keep it from making noise, tape your keys together to keep them from clanging, and we'll get you out of here." He trusted and listened to us.

Several of us then took him out a back window of the modular unit. Slowly, we made our way to the front entrance of the prison, two of us on each side of him. He looked like just another inmate in the middle of the riots.

Around us, turmoil spun a defiant tangle of rubble. Laced with fire and smoke, the voices of rebels floated about like the drops of water on a spider web. Slowly, we made our way, careful that our precious guardian wasn't intercepted by a bloodthirsty spider. We arrived at the front door. "Now we're going to back away," we whispered. "Just open up your shirt and show them you're a guard." Shots rang out overhead. The officer threw open his shirt to reveal his true identity. Immediately, the door opened and our guard was pulled to safety. Mission accomplished!

> **THE ANGELS OF GOD SURROUNDED US**

There were other guards saved in there, too. Not one person died in that riot. Out of thousands of inmates, over two hundred were arrested and charged – that small five percent, blinded with arrogance and hatred. They thought they were so slick! They had these hoods on to cover their identities. But then they would go around a corner and pull their hoods down to smoke. Meanwhile, helicopters overhead would grab a close-up shot of each offender. Busted slick!

Today, our modular unit stands as a testimony of God's grace and favor. There were sixty people housed in that unit. When the riot erupted, forty five of us were Christians.

Months ahead of time, God supernaturally moved all of us down there to be together. We took over that modular unit for God.

And he put a godly officer in charge on that fateful day. And his life was spared for his godly heart towards mankind. Even though we were inmates, he loved us.

Then the state police came to the jail. They did a clean sweep from one end to the other. They handcuffed all of us behind our backs.

Now I've been in enough handcuffs that I can slip out of them in a matter of seconds. But in the middle of that riot, I obediently stood there in those cramped cuffs, singing and praising God.

"You, come over here." I looked up to see one of the state troopers beckoning me towards him. "Yes sir?" I asked as I faced him. Listen he instructed me, "I just want you to tell your group over there to keep singing, praying, and praising God."

"And pray for us," he asked. "Not every trooper here knows God." "Are you a born again believer?" I inquired. "Yes, I am," he replied. "All right," I smiled. "I appreciate that. We will be praying for you guys."

But as I went to step away, he persisted, "I want you to stay here for a minute." His face was tired and drawn, but his eyes intently sought something from me. "I want to share something with you in confidence," he said,. And then he shared some personal sin in his life. With an inmate in handcuffs in the midst of a riot, a trooper confessed his own struggles. I prayed for him and went back to my group.

> **PRAY FOR US, NOT EVERY TROOPER KNOWS GOD**

Shortly after that conversation, the officers began to move all of the inmates to one big yard within the north side of the prison. Now that the police had gained control of the jail, they began to bring all of the inmates back into a cellblock.

One inmate at a time, they would carry you down through the cell block, throw you against a wall, strip you down, and then shackle you together with three other inmates and place you in a cell.

When they carried me in, I was prepared to be abused and manhandled, but one of the officers carrying me through the cellblock leaned into me and whispered, "Jim, we know what you did for the officer. Just relax and cooperate and everything will be fine."

They put me down gently. The officer pointed toward the wall, "Now walk over there." They didn't throw me or drop me against the wall. Then they came over to the wall and gently searched me.

"Okay, now we're going to walk you up to your cell, Jim. We're going to put you in with three of your Christian brothers." And as I turned to walk up, there was that state trooper I had the conversation with in the other section of the prison on the top tier holding a gun, giving me a heads up. I thought I would never see him again, being in a major riot on the other side of the jail. But God had him right there watching over me!

Christmas was coming up soon and Christmas Eve day was the first time they allowed any visiting since the riot broke out. We didn't have showers for two or three weeks.

We had one roll of toilet paper for four people each week. Supplies were low, but that didn't mean our commitment to Jesus had to be.

We were leading people to Jesus on toilet paper. Talk about sacrifices! But they were moving people all around our cell and then shipping them out. Muslims, atheists, people that didn't know Christ, people that were backsliding. We'd write scriptures on the paper and send them out. We were just sharing the gospel. We were chained. We were singing and praising God like in the book of Acts.

## Chapter Ten

### THE EXODUS – FREEDOM AT LAST

Before the prison riot erupted, I was not very well liked or trusted by the prison security officers due to my illegal activities within the prison. But, after the riot, God allowed me to be one of the first of many inmates released from twenty-four hour lock-down to help do repairs throughout the prison.

Because of my faithfulness, I was out of the cell and helping to repair the jail! God had me going from block to block on a plumbing tradesman's instructor crew, with a great boss who was a born again Christian, John McCarty who allowed me to share Christ with anybody and everybody around me, including more officers and troopers.

They saw the fruit. I had participated in helping save an officer's life. My life was changed now. People actually trusted me! And there weren't too many people that could be trusted after the riot. I was given a "Second Chance." You reap what you sow.

Then, one year to the day of the riot, I was released from prison on October 25, 1990. Many people in the local community were worried about another riot; an "anniversary" uprising.

As an "insider" to the story of that fateful time, the day I walked out of that prison, I was interviewed on three major local television news reports, one of them live right across the street from the prison that I walked out of that same day.

> **I WAS GIVEN A SECOND CHANCE**

Then just a few days later on my first Sunday morning attending the local church where the pastors who had visited me in prison were on staff, I was asked by the Senior Pastor to share my testimony with the congregation during both services.

During this time, the church services were being recorded for television, and then aired on a local news television station the following Sunday morning.

Between my sharing my testimony that morning and when the church service aired the following week, there came such a big response from individuals calling in and asking for me to speak with their, sons, daughters, nephews, grandchildren, that the Senior Pastor recognized a call of God on my life.

He then approached the church board members and Elders suggesting that they place me on the church staff working alongside the Pastor in the prison ministry. So within two weeks of being released from prison, I was employed in full time ministry. Incredible! Only God!

I found out that when I shared my testimony on that first Sunday back in society at Christ Community Church, located in Camp Hill, Pennsylvania, that their services were video recorded each week and then aired the following Sunday morning on the local television station.

My wife Doris, now of over twenty-two years, was not at the service the day I spoke, but on the following Sunday she had turned it on at her home to listen and hear what she had missed the week before.

As she heard a different voice other than the Pastor, she began to focus on who I was and what I was saying. She thought to herself, this guy's real. She finished getting ready and headed off to church.

After serving nine years straight in prison, I was a little lonely for female companionship, and that second Sunday after the service as I was up front talking with others, I looked over and saw this godly looking little five-foot one blonde standing there. So I went up to her and said,, "I haven't met you yet, what's your name?"

"Doris," she replied. "What's yours?" "Well, they call me Murphy," and as I started to say more, "no, no," she broke in. "what's your God-given name?" Amazed and taken back, I answered Jim; she then asked me what my last name was. Law I answered, Jim Law.

The following Sunday, Doris approached me and asked if I was interested in making some money by helping her decorate her two businesses she owned. So I went to the pastor I was living with and asked him if it would be alright, and he said, yes, after they meet her and invite her back to their house after church service for lunch.

So after lunch I went with Doris to her place of business to put up Christmas decorations. On the way in her car, I was so nervous. I had not been alone with a woman in nine years. I thought to myself, what do I say? What do I talk about?

It turns out, that she was just as nervous as I was, and I didn't have to worry about what to say, she did all of the talking. She told me her life story on the ride to her business. She was so nervous; she ended up stepping in a cup of coffee that was on the ground in front of her shop. The first signs of love were beginning to blossom. So, at thirty-seven years old I ended up going out with this little blonde.

We went double dating for the first few times as I wanted to honor her and our God. Nine months later, on August 10, 1991 we were married. I did not have much to offer her in the natural, but she'll be the first one to tell you that she married me because she saw Jesus in me. That's the greatest compliment anyone could ever give, I'm blessed and humbled that God would honor me with one of His daughters.

## Chapter Eleven

### THE BLESSINGS AND FAVOR OF GOD

Immediately within three months after release from state prison "I was approved' to teach a Bible study class at the local County prison. Within eight months of my release, I along with my pastor met with the Commissioner of Pennsylvania State Prisons, who is the person appointed by the Governor of the state and oversees all of the state prisons. He gave me a letter giving me permission to enter all of the Pennsylvania State Prisons as someone who is setting a positive role model for other offenders.

That was over twenty-two years ago, and since that first letter, I have had the privilege to meet with every new Secretary of Corrections that is appointed by all newly elected governors and have been given continued permission with an 'updated letter" each time.

In 1994, with the blessing of the church Elders and Pastor, the Lord allowed me to take the prison ministry from out of the church and incorporate it as Second Chance Ministries of Pennsylvania. Since that time I've authored three Faith Based Life Skills curriculums titled, "Walking Your Faith, I, II and III." They consist of teaching inmates the love of God and how He can change their lives for the better through scriptures and life skills. The ministry has grown to be one of the most well-known and respected prison ministries in Pennsylvania ministering in State, County and Federal prisons.

**SETTING A POSITIVE ROLE MODEL**

In 1994 God allowed me to be part of a statewide criminal justice reform task force for Justice Fellowship, the public policy arm of Chuck Colson's Prison Fellowship Ministries. We held nine public hearings across the state interviewing prison chaplains, church leaders, corrections officers, county/city officials and county associations, defense attorneys, district attorneys, educators, ex-offenders/families of offenders, family treatment specialists, inmates, inmate advocates, intermediate punishment program coordinators, judges, juvenile justice, law enforcement, prison ministry workers, prison officials, and probation/parole officials and program directors.

During this time I had the opportunity to meet the then-Attorney General of Pennsylvania. A couple of years later, the Lord allowed me to minister to the Attorney General as he himself stepped down from office and went to prison. He has since turned his life around with God's help and now ministers to others and is a lobbyist for incarcerated men and women.

During these same hearings, I met former Governor of Pennsylvania George M. Leader. A few years later I asked Governor Leader if he would be a speaker at one of our fund raisers for Second Chance Ministries. He agreed and after he spoke at the banquet we met for lunch and he said that he was impressed by what God was doing through the ministry and that he wanted to financially support the ministry through his philanthropy.

The Lord impressed upon him the idea of creating a curriculum that would combine scripture and life skills to train incarcerated individuals to become ministers inside the prisons and that by doing so would be equipped to minister to other incarcerated persons and thereby reducing the workload of the chaplains at each prison. Hence, the Chapel Mentor curriculum was born and later renamed to the Walking Your Faith program.

The Governor financially helped support this program tremendously from its inception until shortly after his death in May, 2013. In the fifteen years of his involvement with Second Chance Ministry and the Walking Your Faith program, over 6,000 individuals graduated the program and had their lives changed for all eternity.

Around 1997 Doris and I were searching for a church to plug into as our home church. I spent a lot of time on Sundays visiting other churches and establishing relationships as a way to make them aware of the ministry that God had allowed me to oversee.

I had heard about a pastor that was known as a man of faith. This man walked and lived by faith, taught the true Word of God, so I desired to meet him. Well, God granted that desire as I was at a dinner event, this Pastor was there and we met. I said, to him that I had heard about him, and he said, to me that he had heard about me also. So we both chuckled and made plans to get together.

I immediately loved his spirit and his genuine faith. What found out was that my wife Doris had become born again through his ministry. So we scheduled a dinner together with our wives. We began to visit his church and ended up staying there as part of his church fellowship for five years, where I was blessed to be an Elder under his leadership.

In 1999 my wonderful and precious wife Doris held a surprise forty-fifth birthday party for me. So in return, wanting to bless her, Doris had told me she really liked a woman teacher on TV, Joyce Meyer. So I scheduled a trip for us to go see her at a church in Virginia Beach, Virginia.

Doris has taught me that whenever you go somewhere, try to sit as close up front as you can so you can pay attention and not be distracted by people in front of you. So when we arrived at the church, which seated 5,000 people, we ended up getting seats in the ministers section on the front row, directly across from Joyce's husband Dave Meyer, and Joyce's brother, David, who was traveling with her ministry at that time.

At the end of the worship time, Joyce took the microphone and began to speak to the audience. As she was speaking, it seemed to me that she kept looking towards Doris and me. I mentioned that to Doris, and Doris said, to me," Oh, stop. She isn't looking at us." Then Joyce walked across the stage, stopped, looked down, pointed at us and said, "The Lord is speaking to me about you two, and I have to be obedient, who are you? Are you two married?" Joyce walked down the steps of the stage and called us forward to stand in front of her. She asked if I was a businessman. I replied that I was in the Lord's business, that I oversee a prison ministry in Pennsylvania.

She said that God told her that we have His favor and blessing. That she sees God providing finances in our life. She then turned and addressed the audience to talk about the importance of prison ministry, how when we go into a prison, that the inmates cannot put money in an offering for our ministry, so she wanted to pray for us and for finances.

> **THE LORD IS SPEAKING TO ME ABOUT YOU TWO**

When Joyce prayed, we had our eyes closed and hands lifted up. As Joyce finished praying for us, she said, now receive it, and we felt her place her hands on each of our foreheads. The power of God went through us and we ended up on the floor. Her husband and brother helped Doris and I up and back to our seats.

Joyce was then explaining to the audience what her ministry does in prisons throughout the country

That eventually they wanted to get permission to go into every state prison in each state of the country. How they provide a bar of soap, a bottle of shampoo and one of her books for every inmate in that prison.

As she continued to talk, I raised my hand and began to wave it attempting to get her attention. Doris asked me," What are you doing"? I said I wanted to tell Joyce what we do in the prisons. Doris was just content to be off the floor and seated again, and was a bit unsettled that I was still continuing to communicate with her in front of all those people after she walked away and back up on the stage.

She reached over and pulled my arm down, but it was too late, Joyce had seen it and walked across the stage and again spoke to me "Is there something you wanted to say to me?" she asked. I said, "Yes, I wanted to share with you what we do in the prisons."

Joyce said, that her ministry had not been in the Pennsylvania prisons as of yet, would I be able to arrange for her ministry to come and distribute her items in Pennsylvania? Absolutely, I responded. She told me to give my information to her husband or her son before we left. It took about a year and a half, but Joyce Meyer ministries came to Pennsylvania, and distributed over 34,000 items to inmates in the state prisons of Pennsylvania.

Since then, Doris and I have had the pleasure of having lunch with Joyce and Dave Meyer when they first started coming to Hershey to hold meetings.

Somewhere around the year 2001 I met and bonded with Pastor Jack Cashman, founder and Senior Pastor of York Christian Fellowship Church in York, Pennsylvania. I was humbled and honored to come alongside him as vice president to incorporate the PA Minister's Association (PMA).

PMA was designed to provide a School of Ministry for those who had the desire to become a licensed or ordained minister, but could not go away to a Bible school for two years or so. It was to equip the everyday lay person in the body of Christ to learn in a practical way how to minister to others.

> **I WAS HUMBLED AND HONORED**

Pastor Jack became a great source of comfort, guidance, wisdom and knowledge for me in my Christian walk.

I truly believe he was one of most Godly men that I have ever met that was tuned in to the Holy Spirit. He went home to be with the Lord in July 2009 at fifty-three years of age due to cancer.

In 2002 in obedience to the Lord, my wife Doris and I planted a church, Light of Hope Community Church. My heart has always been to disciple people in the Word of God, and now I have the privilege to do that each week to a congregation.

God has allowed me to preach the Word of God in churches in Haiti, Mexico, and throughout the United States. I serve as a board member on several ministries, churches and organizations.

I perform numerous wedding ceremonies and funerals. I have been the keynote speaker at fund raisers for ministries. Speak to high school students on the danger of drug and alcohol abuse Hosted a weekly live radio program for ten years, and a television program. Lecture at Messiah College; serve as an adjunct professor at the Philadelphia Lutheran Theological Seminary. Appeared and spoken before the Pennsylvania Senate Judiciary Committee on Crime and Corrections. Lead a team of twenty people on a mission's trip to Haiti, and host a tour in Israel with twenty-two people.

Twenty-five years ago I sat in a state prison cell waiting for a parole slip signed by the Chairman of the Parole Board to see if I was being released back into society. Nowadays, I have lunch and work in collaboration with the Chairman of the Parole Board and his staff, along with the Department of Corrections being allowed to enter all of their prisons throughout Pennsylvania. Look what the Lord has done!

> **GOD HAS ALLOWED ME TO PREACH THE WORD**

What I'm saying is that God can take someone with a back ground like mine and use that person in ways that you could never dream of.

Please understand that I know that everything that has happened to me is because God has caused it to happen. As the Apostle Paul said, in **Galatians 6:14, "But God forbid that I should glory, save in the cross of our Lord Jesus Christ, by whom the world is crucified unto me, and I unto the world."**

## Chapter Twelve

### HOPE FOR THE NEXT GENERATION

After all I have been through in my life, all of the crimes I've committed, all of the hurt and pain I've caused others, I still consider myself a patriotic American.

As I get older and look back at how society has changed since I was a teenager and how the phases I went through were so different compared to the phases teenagers are going through today. I get very concerned. I've been more than a little discouraged about the state of our country over the years. Elections, legislation, Supreme Court decisions, and continued violence have all provided a heavy dose of discouragement to adults and baby boomers like me.

The only hope we have for the next generation is Jesus Christ. The only way a person's life can be changed is through the power of God and the power of what Jesus Christ did at the cross of Calvary and through the power of prayer.

**1Corinthians 1:18** says, *"For the preaching of the cross is to them that perish foolishness; but unto us which are saved it is the power of God."*

Biblical hope involves expectancy, not wishful thinking. Biblical hope consists of waiting for God to accomplish His perfect will in our lives and earnestly expecting Him to come through for you.

We must all ask ourselves the question, "What do I really believe? Do I truly believe that Jesus Christ is who the Bible says He is? If I do, does my lifestyle line up with my beliefs? Am I being a true witness to the youth of today?"

We all have heard testimonies of how people lived their whole lives without a commitment to Christ, and then at some point in time they accepted Jesus Christ as their Lord and Savior. From that moment on their lives were never the same and they share with others how they wished they would have made a commitment to Christ many years before that. The

> **BIBLICAL HOPE INVOLVES EXPECTANCY**

same is true no matter what age the person is. Teenagers need to hear more life changing testimonies and parents need to encourage them to seek God for themselves and explain to them the reality of God and the reality of evil. Parents need to spend more time with their children and set a godlier example in the home before evil overcomes their children.

When you invest time into a young person's life, you're investing in not only their future, but the future of America.

Hope for the next generation starts with you living a hope filled life through Jesus Christ and then bringing that hope to others. Will you take the challenge? Have you accepted Jesus Christ as your Lord and Savior? If not, please continue reading with an open heart. If you have already accepted Jesus Christ as your Lord and Savior, share this book with someone who has not and pray for them daily.

## Salvation Prayer

### 1. God loves you and has a plan for you!

The Bible says, "God so loved the world that He gave His one and only Son, [Jesus Christ], that whoever believes in Him shall not perish, but have eternal life" (John 3:16). Jesus said, "I came that they may have life and have it abundantly" — a complete life full of purpose (John 10:10).

**But here's the problem:**

### 2. Man is sinful and separated from God.

We have all done thought or said bad things, which the Bible calls "sin." The Bible says, "All have sinned and fall short of the glory of God" (Romans 3:23). The result of sin is death, spiritual separation from God (Romans 6:23).

**But here's the good news:**

### 3. God sent His Son to die for your sins!

Jesus died in our place so we could live with Him in eternity.
"God demonstrates His own love toward us, in that while we were yet sinners, Christ died for us" (Romans 5:8). But it didn't end with His death on the cross. He rose again and still lives! "Christ died for our sins. ... He was buried. ... He was raised on the third day, according to the Scriptures." (1 Corinthians 15:3-4). Jesus is the only way to God.
Jesus said, "I am the way, and the truth, and the life; no one comes to the Father, but through Me" (John 14:6)

### 4. Would you like to receive God's forgiveness?

We can't earn salvation; we are saved by God's grace when we have faith in His Son, Jesus Christ. All you have to do is believe you are a sinner, and that Jesus Christ died for your sins, and ask His forgiveness. He knows you and loves you no matter what you have done.

What matters to Him is the attitude of your heart, your honesty. I suggest praying the following prayer to accept Christ as your Savior:

**"Dear Lord Jesus,**

**I acknowledge and confess that I have sinned against You according to Your Word, and I ask You for Your forgiveness. I believe Jesus that You died for my sins and rose again in resurrection life. I ask that You come into my heart and life. Fill me with the Holy Spirit and baptize me with your power. Help me to live each day in obedience to Your Word as much as I can with Your help. I trust and follow You as my Lord and Savior. Guide my life and help me to do your will.
In Jesus name, amen."**

If you prayed this prayer with a sincere heart, you are now born again and a child of God. Be sure to immediately tell others what you have done. Start attending a church that preaches and teaches the true Word of God along with Jesus Christ and Him crucified. Then write me or call me and let me know.

Jim Law
100 Floral Lane
Dauphin, PA 17018
717-921-2622.